# Thistle Goes for a Ride

Lady Thistle, the Horse
BOOK SIX

## D.H. ANDERSON
### Illustrations by STEVEN LESTER

# Thistle Goes for a Ride

Paperback ISBN 978-1-960007-75-9
HardBack ISBN 978-1-960007-76-6
eBOOK ISBN 978-1-960007-77-3

Published by
**Little Blessing Books**
an imprint of
Orison Publishers, Inc.
PO Box 188, Grantham, PA 17027
www.OrisonPublishers.com

## Acknowledgments

Contributing Veterinarian: Apryle Horbal, VMD

Lady Thistle, a thoroughbred filly who was born at Waterdam Farm, has always been at her mother, Polly's, side. At six months old, she still drinks Mom's milk but she also eats lots of grass, grain, and hay. She is growing fast, and it is time for her to face a new challenge.

Thistle must learn to be on her own, and Polly must learn to accept that her baby is growing up.

Farmhands prepare a separate stall for Thistle right across from Polly's, so Polly and Thistle can see each other.

5

They choose two fields with a narrow path between them.

The next morning, farmhands take Daphne, Wynter, and Lite to their fields. Then they lead Thistle and Polly out of the barn. Polly enters the field with Daphne, and the gate is closed behind her, keeping Thistle outside. Thistle and Polly look upset.

8

When Thistle is led to the next gate, she cries to Polly that something is very wrong! Thistle knows Wynter and Lite, but this is not her field! Thistle's eyes go from worried to frightened, and Polly paces nervously along the fence.

Lite nickers to Thistle to follow him into his field. Wynter goes to his favorite grassy spot. In the other field, Polly whinnies to her foal, and Daphne tries to calm her. But Thistle panics and runs right through the fences, back to her mother's side.

Dr. Apryle and the workers are close by, and they grab a halter and rope to catch Thistle. They put the fence rails back into place.

10

Apryle and the workers keep Thistle and Polly away from the fences until they are finally distracted by the delicious grass and begin to graze in their separate fields. Thistle realizes that she is okay.

Lady Thistle grows rapidly over the next two years.
She becomes a horse!

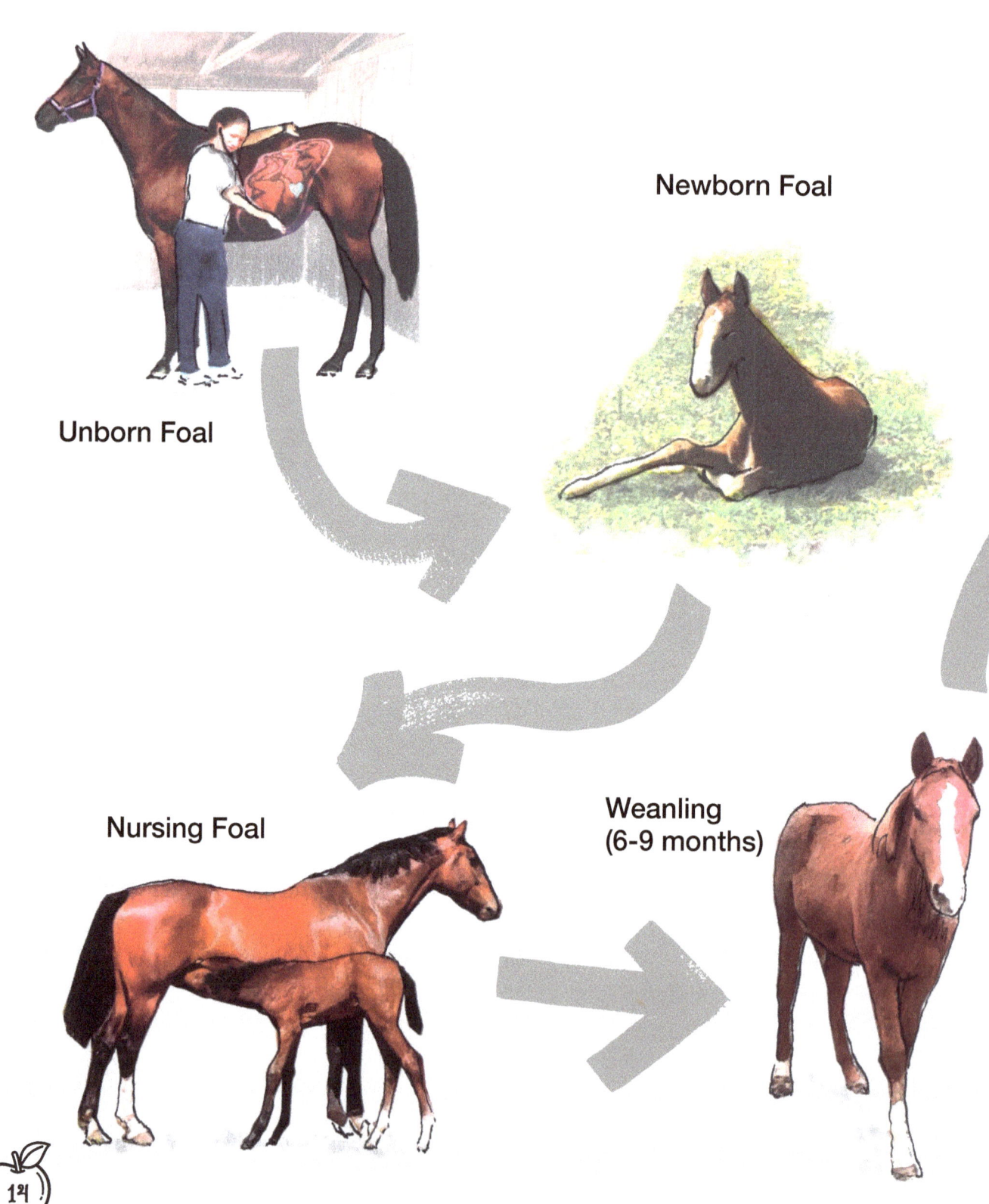

Unborn Foal

Newborn Foal

Nursing Foal

Weanling
(6-9 months)

1와

Yearling Filly

Adult Mare
(Over 4 years old)

15

The sweet, green grass of the pasture is a pleasure every day as Thistle grazes. Lite tells her that like Polly, he was a racehorse and lived at a racetrack. He worked very hard and loved winning races! Wynter shares stories about his days as a show horse. He and Apryle worked hard together and earned ribbons, like Thistle's dad did.

Thistle sees Daphne
and Polly in the riding
ring. They are brushed,
and saddles are put on
their backs. Dr. Apryle
and Mom ride them
in the ring and on the
paths around the farm.
It looks like fun!

Thistle and her family know it's time to decide what kind of horse she will be— a winning racehorse like her mom or a show horse like her dad?

They all agree that Lady Thistle should be a show horse. That way, she can live at Waterdam Farm with the family and her animal friends.

Dr. Apryle calls trainer Blaine. He invites Thistle to his barn, where he will work with her for a few months. He teaches horses small lessons each day, and they calmly learn to enjoy carrying a rider.

Thistle hears that she will have a saddle and a rider on her back.
Another growing-up lesson!

How will Thistle get to the training barn? Horses are moved from place to place in horse trailers and trucks. She must learn to walk up the ramp onto the very scary trailer! Dr. Apryle and her assistant, Taylor, know she will be afraid. And Thistle is big, so they must be cautious. Today's goal is for Thistle to place one foot on the ramp. Thistle is curious, and when she checks out the ramp with her nose, she earns a treat!

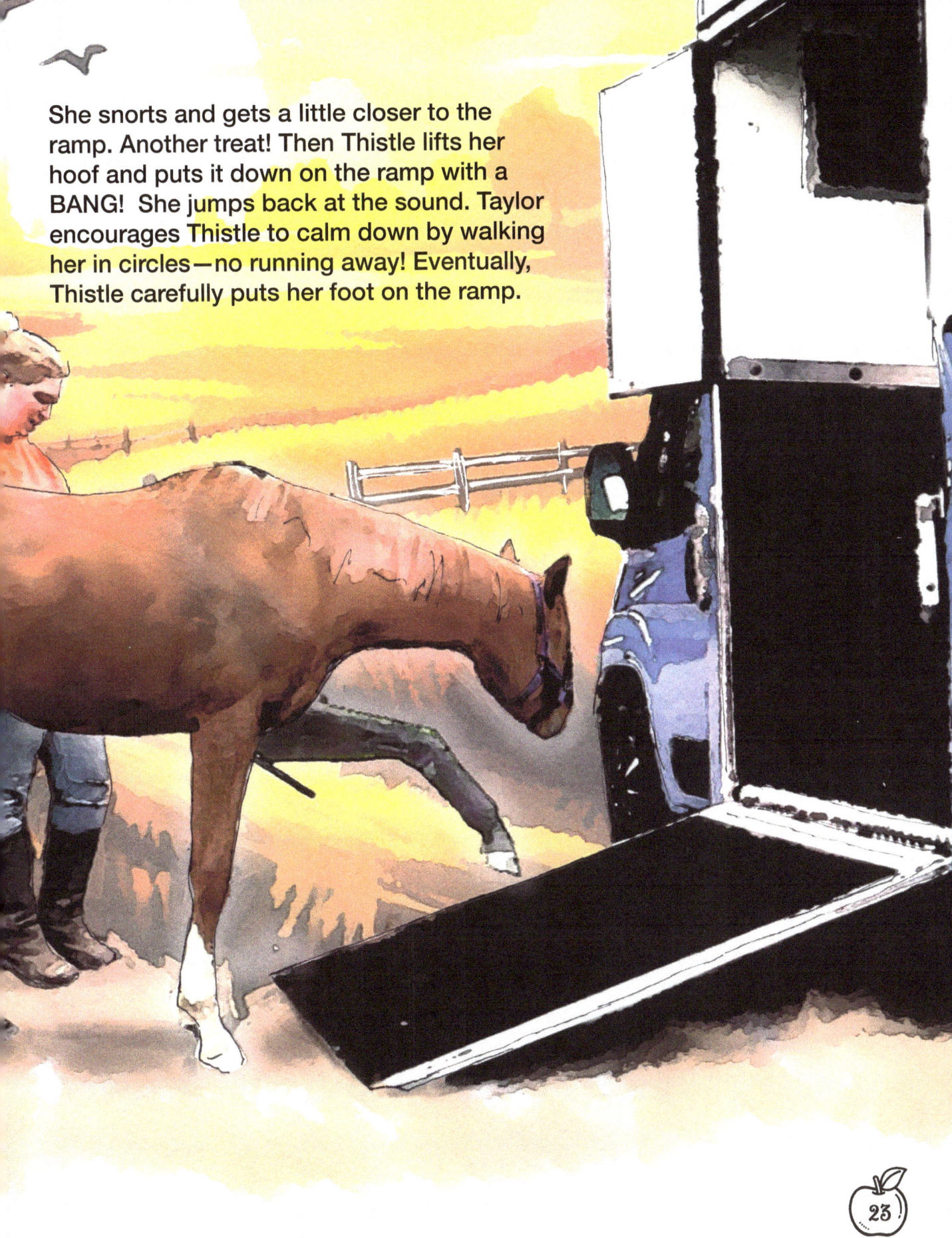

She snorts and gets a little closer to the ramp. Another treat! Then Thistle lifts her hoof and puts it down on the ramp with a BANG! She jumps back at the sound. Taylor encourages Thistle to calm down by walking her in circles—no running away! Eventually, Thistle carefully puts her foot on the ramp.

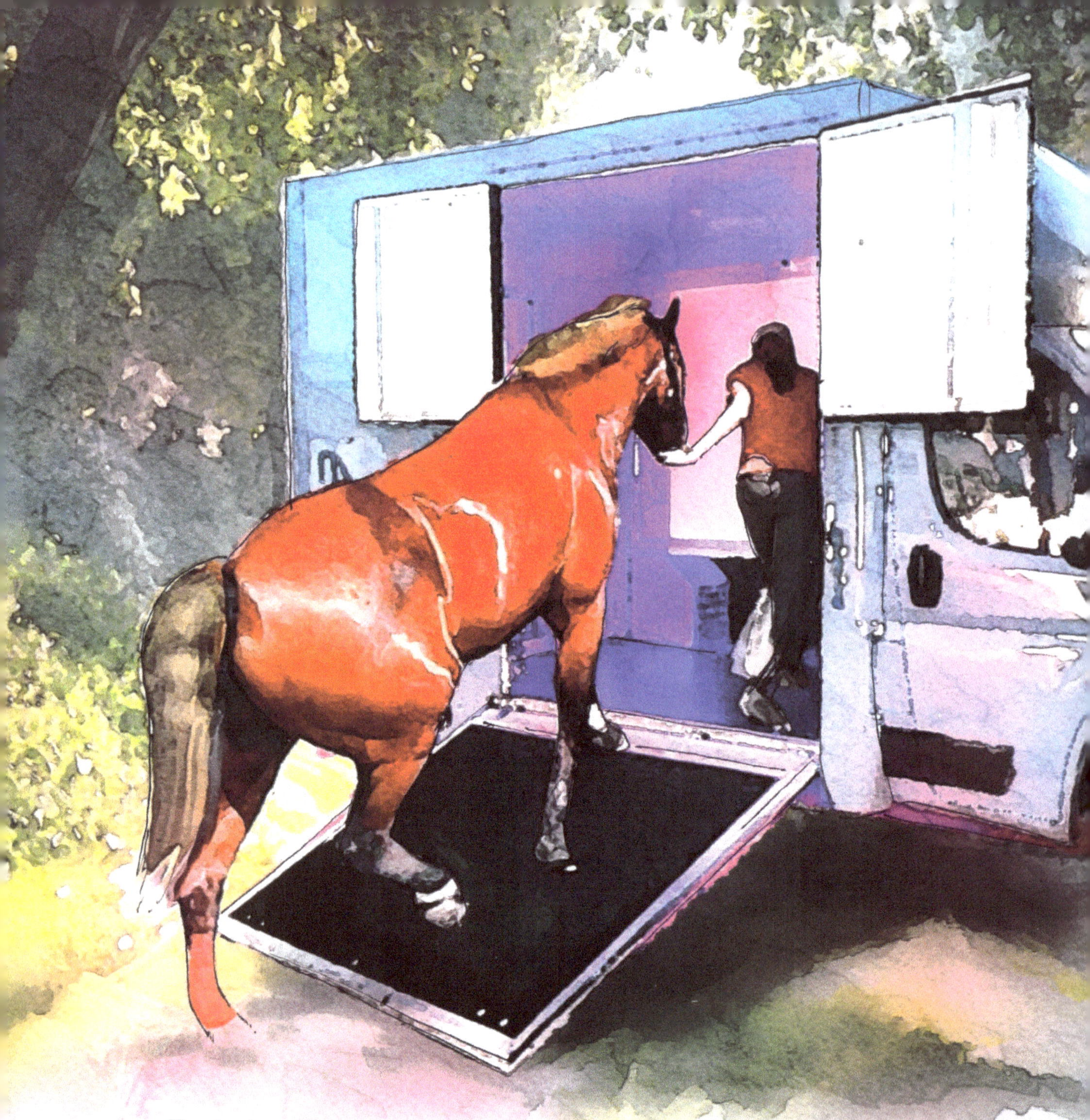

Each day, Taylor leads Thistle to the trailer. She gently encourages her with light taps of a long crop, stopping as soon as Thistle takes a step closer. One foot, two feet, three, and then all four are on the ramp! Soon, Thistle is happily earning her daily treat! On the final training day, Dr. Apryle and Taylor place hay in the trailer. As Thistle walks up the ramp, she sees the hay, feels safe, and walks right into position for her ride.

They call trainer Blaine and tell
him they are on their way.

That evening, the other horses are concerned when they enter the barn and Thistle is not with them. Polly is upset, but Daphne reminds her that Thistle is growing up. Finally, Polly eats her grain.

The barn is closed for the night with the calming sound of horses munching hay.

# Did You Know...?

Like all pets (puppies, kittens, and other animals) foals must learn to be independent of their mothers much earlier in their lives than human children do. This is called "weaning."

The best age to wean a foal is usually around six months. The foal must be able to eat grass, grain, and hay and rely less on mother's milk for nutrition. The foal's health, maturity, and growth are considered, as well as the temperament of the mare. Some mares are more comfortable around humans and pass that attitude along to their foals.

Experienced horse handlers know that preparing proper spaces both in the barn and outside is necessary to minimize the stress for the mother, her baby, and the human family. A separate stall that is close and allows the foal and mom to see and smell each other makes their separation less frightening. In the fields, fences must prevent the mare and foal from rejoining but also be safe in case they try to breach the barrier. Close monitoring is important. If an injury or other problem is observed, a veterinarian or experienced trainer should be contacted.

Horse-breeding farms wean their foals in groups, but they, too, allow a period of time for the mares and foals to have visual and smell contact.

All horses must learn to walk onto a trailer so they can be moved to a different farm, go to a park for a trail ride, attend a show or competition, or in case an emergency arises.

Loading onto and off a trailer is a unique challenge for horses, and it should be practiced when they are young. Most important is the safety of the horse and the handler. An experienced handler encourages the horse with positive reinforcement to overcome its fear of the ramp and the close quarters of the trailer. For every positive response—even one step toward the trailer—the horse is rewarded and allowed to pause and take in its surroundings. Then, one more step. Each horse responds differently, and the process cannot be rushed. It will most likely will take days of practice!

Horses can be trained to step forward or backward in response to a "clicker" tool used by the handler or a "tickle" on the shoulder or hindquarter from a long-handled crop. This helps in lots of different situations, including loading on a trailer.

If a horse loads and is comfortable, it will lick and chew, a sign of understanding. Some horses even become excited to ride on a trailer for a new experience!

**BOOK ONE**

**BOOK TWO**

**BOOK THREE**

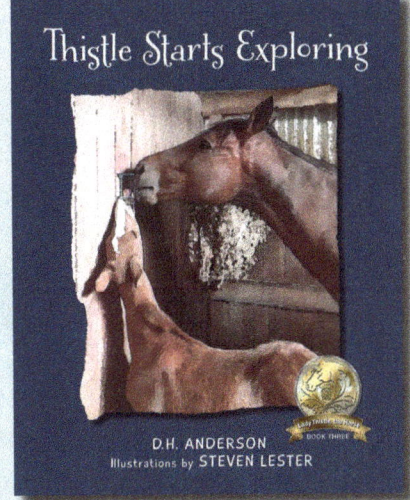

**BOOK FOUR**

**BOOK FIVE**

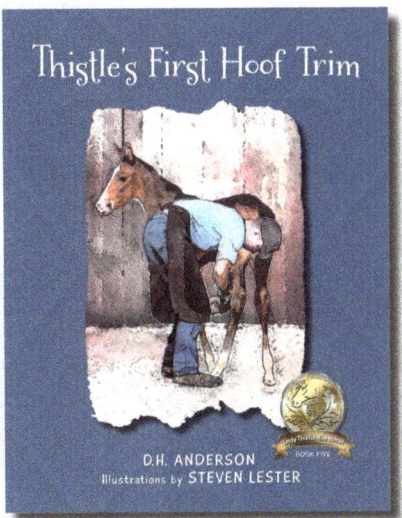

Watch for Lady Thistle's Journey to continue.

SCAN ME

www.ingramcontent.com/pod-product-compliance
Lightning Source LLC
Chambersburg PA
CBHW041132120626
46547CB00019B/2954